YOUR Amazing
BRAIN
and how it works

Insight into the structure
and activity of the brain

Marge Engelman

By Marge Engelman
Edited by Joni Nygard
Graphic Design by Jennifer Conn
Photos by Sarah Elizabeth Sprague,
pgs. 3, 10, 11, 18, 20–23, 26.

An Attainment Company Publication
©2008 Attainment Company, Inc., All rights reserved.
Printed in China
ISBN: 1-57861-650-6

Attainment Company, Inc.

P.O. Box 930160
Verona, Wisconsin 53593-0160 USA
1-800-327-4269
www.AttainmentCompany.com

How is it that you can read?
How is it you can talk, walk, and dance?

You are able to do all of these things and much more because of your **brain.**

How does your **memory** work? How do **alcohol** and **coffee** affect your brain? How can you keep your brain healthy as you **get older**?

The brain is the manager of your body. It responds to your behavior and your every day actions. In many ways it determines who you are.

The average brain weighs about three pounds, about the size of a medium cantaloupe.

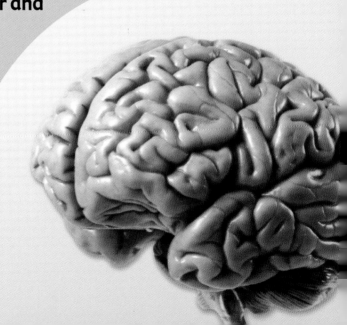

It is highly convoluted, soft and pinkish-gray in color. It is the most complicated piece of equipment in the universe.

The brain fits inside a protective skull made of hard bones.

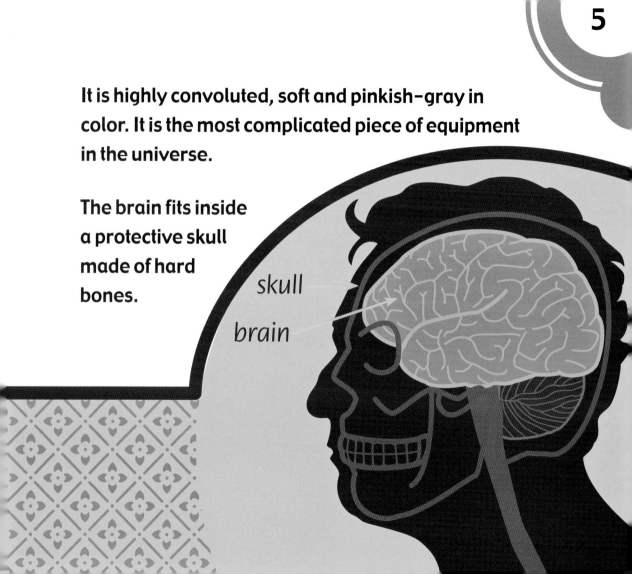

skull

brain

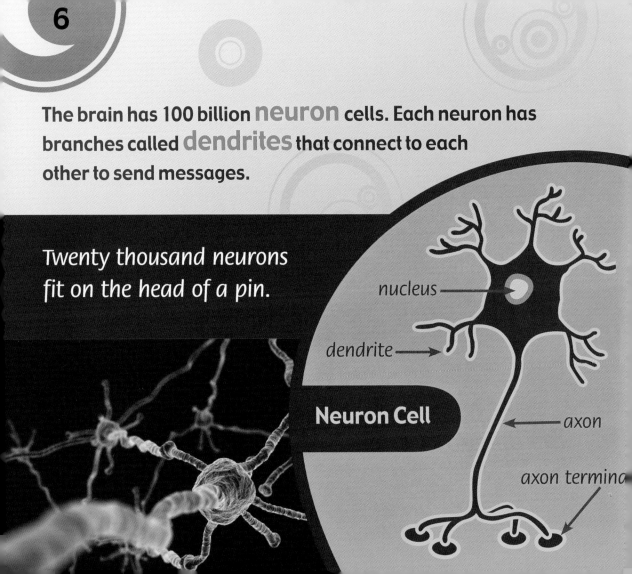

The brain has 100 billion **neuron** cells. Each neuron has branches called **dendrites** that connect to each other to send messages.

Twenty thousand neurons fit on the head of a pin.

nucleus

dendrite

Neuron Cell

axon

axon termina

The human brain can store more information than all the libraries in the world.

There are as many neurons in the brain as there are trees in the Amazon Forests.

The total length of the dendrites would equal 100,000 miles.

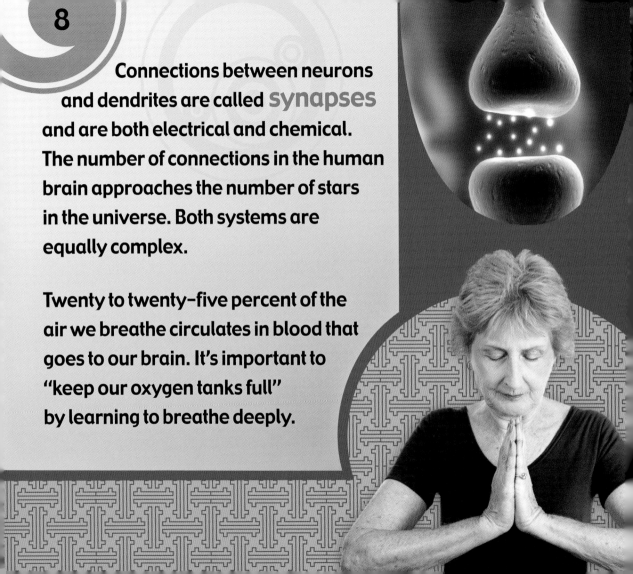

Connections between neurons and dendrites are called **synapses** and are both electrical and chemical. The number of connections in the human brain approaches the number of stars in the universe. Both systems are equally complex.

Twenty to twenty-five percent of the air we breathe circulates in blood that goes to our brain. It's important to "keep our oxygen tanks full" by learning to breathe deeply.

The **mind** is what the brain does—it's sometimes described as software running on the hardware of the brain.

Different parts of the brain are responsible for various functions.

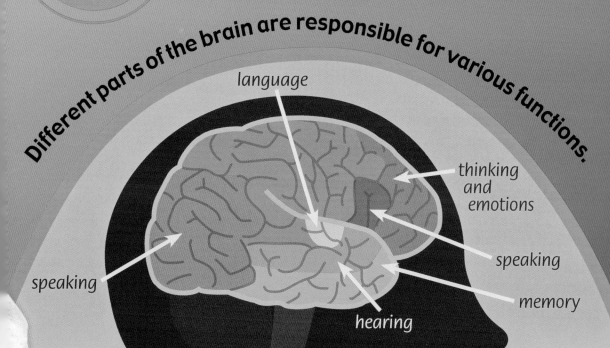

language

thinking and emotions

speaking

speaking

memory

hearing

The **right** side of the brain controls the **left** side of the body and vice versa.

Our **memory** is housed in the brain. We have short term and long term memory and within each of those there are different categories. For example, we use our "procedural memory" without thinking about it. You automatically remember how to tie your shoes, walk, and ride a bike.

Many factors can affect your memory: physical and mental activity, diet, medical conditions, fatigue, depression, anxiety, stress, information overload.

The brain is also where our moods and feelings originate. Liquids called neurotransmitters bathe the neurons and affect how we feel.

The **cerebrum** makes up 85% of the brain's weight and is the reasoning part of the brain. It allows you to do math problems, feed your fish, dance, remember family birthdays and draw pictures.

The **cerebellum** is at the back of the brain below the cerebrum. It controls movement, balance and coordination.

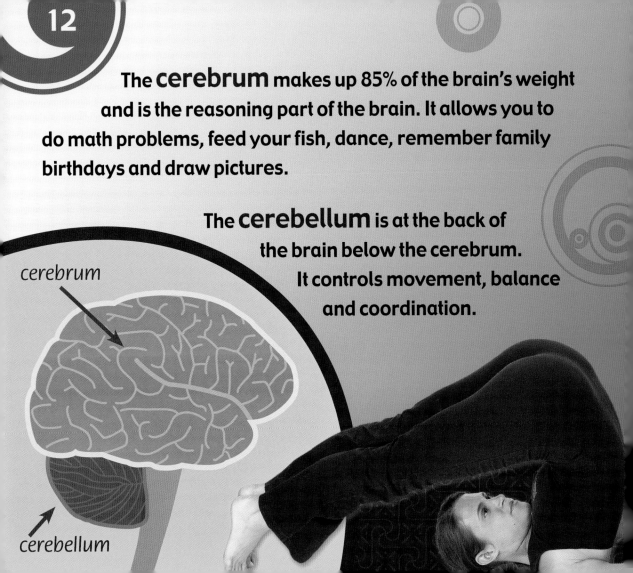

cerebrum

cerebellum

The frontal lobe governs decision making, problem solving and planning.

The parietal lobe receives and processes sensory information.

The occipital lobe controls vision, identifies colors and recognizes words.

The temporal lobe manages memory, emotion, hearing and language.

parietal

frontal

occipital

temporal

The brain has four main lobes

Deep within the brain is the **hippocampus.**
This organ has to do with memory and learning.

The **corpus callosum** is a thick membrane separating the two halves of the brain. The left brain and right brain tend to have different functions.

The **left** hemisphere tends to deal with words, numbers, logic, and rational thinking.

The **right** hemisphere handles abstract thinking, emotions, creativity, intuition, and color.

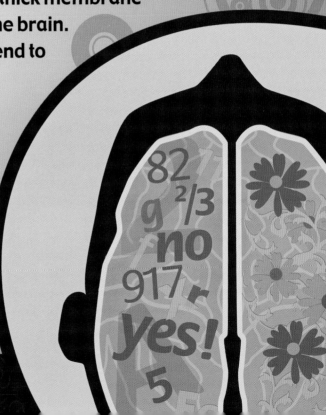

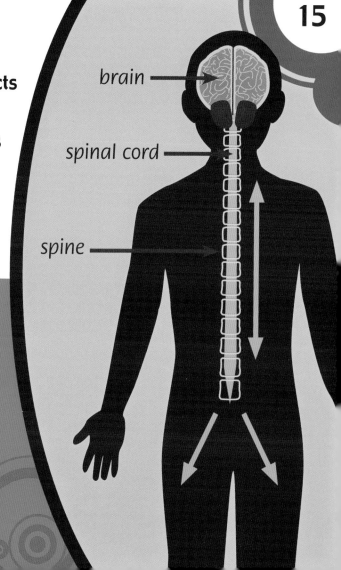

The **brain stem** connects the brain and **spinal cord,** sending messages back and forth between the brain and other parts of the body.

Your brain controls all the functions necessary for **staying alive** such as breathing air, digesting food, and circulating blood.

brain

spinal cord

spine

The brain is busy sending and receiving millions of messages every day. Sleep gives it a chance to regroup and consolidate information.

Now that we have technology such as PET scans and fMRI (functional Magnetic Resonance Imagery) we can look inside the brain to see how it works and begin to understand how people feel and think.

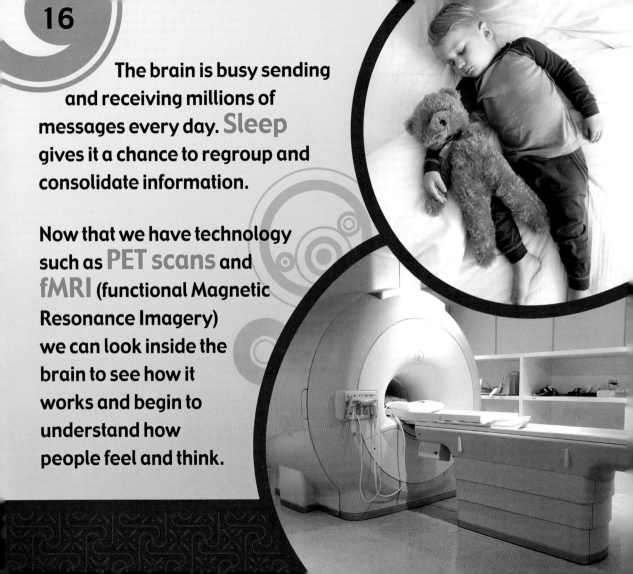

We are learning that the brain is very pliable and can change even in old age; indeed some parts of the brain can generate new neurons. Creating new brain cells is called **neurogenesis**.

We do lose some neurons as we age, but with 100 billion in stock, the loss is insignificant. A little slowing of thoughts and memory normally occurs with growing older.

How we use our minds has a lot to do with how we age. The brain can ALWAYS learn. Just like our bodies, our brain also needs **exercise**.

Boredom is the brain's cry for action!

Keeping our minds active by doing a variety of mental exercises can improve our memory, reasoning, and speed of thinking.

It is important to learn to do new things, rather than continuing to perform already-learned skills.

Great **mental workouts** to try:

- ◎ Read—books, newspapers, magazines

- ◎ Write—letters, a diary, stories, poetry, email

- ◎ Play a musical instrument

- ◎ Sing, whistle, dance

- ◎ Have a hobby—painting, pottery, knitting, quilting, wood working, bird watching

- ◎ Play word and number games—crossword puzzles, Jumbles, Scrabble, Sudoku

- ◎ Plan a trip

- Play cards—bridge, pinochle, euchre, 500, canasta

- Use a computer—get on the internet, send and receive email

- Memorize—telephone numbers, social security numbers, names, birthdays, poetry, famous quotes, jokes

- Volunteer for a cause you care about

- Join a book club or study group

- Plan a party and invite the neighbors

The brain craves **innovation**.

Many researchers now believe doing mental exercise can reduce the risk of Alzheimer's Disease and other dementias and maintain brain health as we age.

It may take longer to learn and store new information, so concentration becomes increasingly important. But even into old age, the brain continues to fine tune itself in response to new learning and experiences.

Recent research indicates that we can "train our minds and thus change our brains."

Our body's **genes** are powerful and do set some limits on what we can achieve mentally and physically. However, genes are highly sensitive to what we perceive, the emotions we feel, and many other factors. So we do have a great deal of control over most of our brain health.

The brain still is developing during the teen years. Recent research suggests drinking alcohol during these years may damage vulnerable areas in the brain. Teens and young adults who drank heavily over a period of time have caused shrinkage in an area of the brain responsible for memory and learning.

Wine may be beneficial in modest amounts, but heavy consumption of any kind of alcohol is detrimental to the brain.

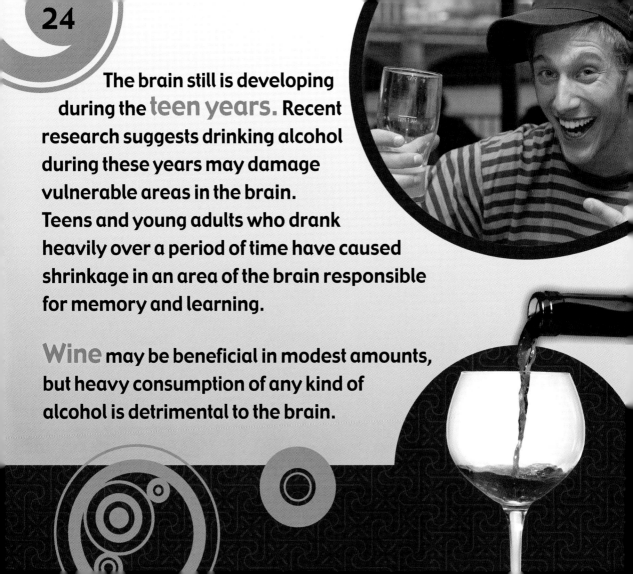

Older brains may be **wiser** than younger brains because they've had more time in which to learn, and in the process created more neural connections. Verbal abilities often improve with age. Older brains tend to use both hemispheres at once, helping to keep them **sharp**. Reasoning and problem solving are still essentially intact.

Brain imaging (fMRI and PET Scans) shows less evidence of fear, anger, discontent, and hatred than in younger adults. This results in being more at **peace** with one's self and the world.

*In some ways, brain function **improves** with age.*

In addition to stimulating mental activity, it's good to:

- ◎ Be physically active

- ◎ Eat a wholesome diet

- ◎ Engage in conversations with a wide variety of people: family, friends and strangers

- ◎ Meditate to reduce stress and anxiety

- ◎ Do things that are new and different

- ◎ Drink plenty of water

- ◎ Cultivate a spiritual practice

The best news of all is that now there is virtual agreement that the brain is capable of **positive change** throughout our lives, even into old age.

Our brains are **truly amazing!**

Glossary

In order of appearance in the text

brain—The part of the central nervous system that is located within the skull. The body's primary receiver, organizer and distributor of information.

skull—The collection of bones encasing the brain and giving form to the head and face.

neuron—A nerve cell in the brain that sends and receives electrical and chemical signals over long distances within the body.

dendrite—A tree-like extension of the neuron cell body. It receives information from other neurons.

synapse—A gap between two neurons that functions as the site of information transfer in the brain.

cerebrum—The largest part of the brain. It is divided into two hemispheres. Each hemisphere is divided into four lobes. It is considered the base of conscious mental process.

cerebellum—The portion of the brain in the back of the head between the cerebrum and the brain stem, the second largest structure in the brain.

frontal lobe—The portion of the brain that governs decision making, problem solving and planning.

parietal lobe—The portion of the brain that receives and processes sensory information from the body.

occipital lobe—The part of the brain that controls vision.

temporal lobe—The portion of the brain that manages memory, emotion, hearing, and language.

hippocampus—The seahorse-shaped organ deep in the brain that is involved in memory, learning, and emotion.

corpus callosum—The large bundle of nerve fibers linking the left and right hemispheres of the brain.

neurogenesis—The recently discovered ability of the brain to regenerate new brain cells.

PET scans—The popular name and abbreviation of Positive Emission Tomography, a procedure in which a small amount of glucose is injected into a vein and a scanner makes pictures of what it sees.

fMRI—The popular name and abbreviation of functional Magnetic Resonance Imagery, a test using a magnet linked to a computer to create pictures of areas inside the body.

neurotransmitter—
A chemical released by neurons at a synapse to relay information.

short-term memory—
A phase of memory that is short-lived with information stored for only several seconds to several minutes.

long-term memory—
A phase of memory in which information storage may last from hours to a lifetime.

procedural memory—The long-term memory of skills and procedures, or "how to" knowledge, such as the ability to ride a bicycle.

Alzheimer's Disease— A progressive neurologic disease of the brain that leads to the irreversible loss of neurons. The hallmarks are progressive impairment in memory, judgment, decision making, orientation to physical surroundings and language.

dementia—The progressive decline in cognitive function due to damage or disease in the brain beyond what might be expected from normal aging.

genes—Units of hereditary information unique to each person.

Resources

To learn more about how the brain works and how to keep it healthy, these selected resources may be helpful.

Books and Card Sets

Mental Fitness Cards, *Marge Engelman, Attainment Company, 2001.*

Whole Brain Workouts, *Marge Engelman, Attainment Company, 2006.*

The Mature Mind, the Positive Power of the Aging Brain, *Gene D. Cohen, Basic Books, 2005.*

Dental Floss for the Mind, A Complete Program for Boosting Your Brain Power, *Michael Noir, and Bernard Croisile, McGraw Hill, 2005.*

Making a Good Brain Great, The Amen Clinic Program for Achieving and Sustaining Optimal Mental Performance, Daniel G. Amen, Harmony Books, 2005.

Train Your Mind, Change Your Brain: How a New Science Reveals Our Extraordinary Power to Transform Ourselves, Sharon Begley, (Forward by the Dalai Lama), Ballantine Books, 2007.

The Brain that Changes Itself, Norman Doidge, Viking, 2007.

How Does Your Brain Work?, Don L. Curry, Scholastic, Inc. 2003.

New Technology

Healthy Brain Kit—Clinically Proven Tools to Boost Your Memory, Sharpen Your Mind, Keep Your Brain Young. Comes in a box with two audio CDs, 35 brain training cards, 52 page workbook for about $30.00, Andrew Weil and Gary Small, Sounds True, 2007.

Nintendo DSL Program: Brain Age—The hardware is a little hand held piece, costs about $130; the program costs about $20.

Posit Science Brain Fitness Program—To read more go to the web and type in "Posit Science Brain Fitness News." Program sells for about $400 and has the most research to back up its benefits. Used in numerous senior centers.

Mindfit, Brain Power Fitness Software—A program to better your memory and brain functioning. Program sells for about $150 and is claimed to be the most fun to use.

Web Sites

My Brain Trainer. *A website based program. $9.95 for annual membership.* www.mybraintrainer.com

American Society on Aging—*MindAlert.* www.asaging.org/mindalert

Aerobics of the Mind—**Engelman.** www.agenet.com

Keep Your Brain Alive—**Katz.** www.neurobics.com

American Association of Retired People Magazine www.aarpmagazine.org/games

Tetris. www.online-game.tv/play/tetris

Mental Fitness—*Card sets and books.* www.AttainmentCompany.com

There are new web sites popping up everywhere. Search words like: "mental fitness," "brain games," "keeping sharp," or "puzzles."